Original title:
Untamed Verses

Copyright © 2025 Creative Arts Management OÜ
All rights reserved.

Author: Penelope Hawthorne
ISBN HARDBACK: 978-1-80566-705-6
ISBN PAPERBACK: 978-1-80566-990-6

Reckless Rhyme

Once a cat in a hat so high,
Said, 'I can dance; watch me fly!'
Tripped on a shoe, fell with a thud,
Landed right smack in a puddle of mud.

A dog with a bone thought it quite cute,
Joined in the dance with a wiggly root.
Both laughed and rolled, what a silly sight,
In their wild world, everything felt right.

Heartbeats of the Untamed

A squirrel on a branch sang a tune,
While bouncing around like a silly buffoon.
Doves joined in, flapping wings in glee,
As they danced with the leaves, oh so carefree.

A turtle watched, with a slow, lazy glance,
Said, 'I'd join, but I can't find my pants!'
The animals chuckled, in laughter they swayed,
In their heartbeats of chaos, joy wouldn't fade.

Fractured Monologues

A goldfish once spoke of a dream so grand,
To run through the fields, not just swim in sand.
But each time it tried, it flopped on the floor,
With a splash and a sigh, it returned to the shore.

A parrot nearby mimicked its plight,
'Just flap your fins, you'll take off in flight!'
But gills don't help when you're on dry land,
It's hard being fish in a world so unplanned.

Serendipity in Scrawls

A rabbit with glasses wrote notes in the dirt,
Of all the wild zucchinis that led to dessert.
But scribbling too fast, it tripped on a stone,
And all of its wisdom flew straight to the bone.

An owl perched nearby gave a wise little hoot,
'You can't eat your thoughts, stick to the root!'
Yet in the wild chaos, they found laughs and fun,
With scrawls full of dreams, their day was well done.

Verses from the Edge

A squirrel stole my sandwich, oh dear,
It danced on the grass, full of cheer.
I laughed as it leapt, a nutty ballet,
Who knew lunch could run away in such a way?

The pigeons all gathered, a feast they sought,
With breadcrumbs of wisdom, they loosely taught.
They cooed a soft tune like a strange serenade,
While I pondered my choices, my meal betrayed.

Roaming in Rhythms

A cat in a hat juggled three tied flies,
While thinking he'd conquer the kitchen pies.
He slipped on a mat, oh the drama, what fun!
The pigeons applauded his fall, one by one.

Dancing with spoons, the dishes chimed loud,
The floor turned into a curious crowd.
And there on the table, a cake spun around,
As forks started prancing with rhythm profound.

Unruly Sonnets

A frog in a suit went to join a rock band,
He croaked in the mic with a cane in his hand.
The lizards were grooving, the ants formed a line,
As gophers spun records, all feeling divine.

Jellybeans tossed, a sweet flying spree,
Lollipops drummed, what a sight to see!
The stage made of mushrooms, a dream come alive,
For a night full of laughter, oh how we thrived!

Fragments of Freedom

In a marmalade jar, a frog built a throne,
He ruled over toast like a king all alone.
With jellybean courtiers all dancing away,
His reign was as sticky as a bright sunny day.

Chickens on scooters, they raced down the lane,
With feathers a-flap, oh what a refrain!
They clucked and they chuckled, a parade in full swing,
Proclaiming the chaos that freedom can bring.

Resounding Risk in Rhyme

I saw a cat wear a tutu,
Dancing under the light of the moon.
The dog clapped paws with delight,
Thinking this was quite the night.

A squirrel tried to steal a hat,
But slipped right onto a mat.
His friends laughed, rolling on the floor,
While he vowed to not try that anymore.

The goldfish jumped out for a swim,
But then got caught in a whim.
He wore a tiny snorkel with pride,
While the kids giggled, unable to hide.

So here's to the wild and the free,
Where laughter flows like a glee.
Life's silly moments bring us cheer,
In this whimsical world, oh dear!

Celebrations of the Uncontrolled

An ant in a suit held a feast,
With cakes and pies for each little beast.
The party was wild, what a sight!
As they danced and laughed into the night.

A frog with a guitar, what a show!
Played tunes as the crowd began to grow.
The crickets sang, adding a hum,
While the bees buzzed to the beat of the drum.

A flamingo tried to do the twist,
But fell over in a pink mist.
Everyone cheered, it was quite a blast,
Creating memories that would ever last.

When the sun began to rise and glow,
The wild revelers began to slow.
But laughter lingered on the breeze,
In this celebration, we feel at ease!

Wilderness in Words

In the forest of my mind,
Words dance around like squirrels,
Chasing each other up trees,
Barking rhymes that give me twirls.

The bushes joke with the breeze,
Tickling whispers in my ear,
My thoughts run wild like deer,
Leaping over doubt and fears.

Vines tangle up my sentences,
Creating knots I can't untie,
But laughter rings through the branches,
Soaring high into the sky.

A bear in a bowtie walks by,
With a top hat askew on his head,
He winks and laughs at my plight,
And offers me a slice of bread.

Breakaway Beats

A drum in the distance calls,
As I stumble through the leaves,
Beats bounce off the tall pines,
Making even the owls wheeze.

The rabbits clap their little paws,
While the fox plays the tambourine,
Dancing shadows light the night,
In a woodland rave, so keen.

I trip on roots and giggle hard,
A raccoon joins with a grin,
Whiskers twitch, he sways along,
This party's sure to spin!

Bonnets made of clover twist,
As fireflies spin and twirl,
We break away from boredom's grip,
In nature's wild, funny whirl.

Poetic Mayhem

Words spill like paint from a pot,
Colors splattering everywhere,
Giggling lines in a rhyming twist,
Creating chaos without a care.

A flamingo in polka dots,
Sips tea with a bumblebee,
Laughing at the absurdity,
Of this wild verse jamboree.

Raccoons sport chalked-up noses,
As they juggle puns with flair,
Each joke lands with a soft bounce,
And tickles the hedgehog's hair.

Nature's an open mic night,
With every creature taking turns,
The laughter echoes loud and bright,
A lesson in how chaos churns.

Windswept Lines

The wind whips through my thoughts,
With a belly laugh on the way,
It tosses rhymes like confetti,
In a topiary ballet.

Clouds roll in with a chuckle,
As raindrops tap dance on roofs,
Each splash a line of giggles,
In nature's playful grooves.

Kites fly high, tied to dreams,
While squirrels weave through the air,
It's a comic book of breezes,
With adventures laid threadbare.

A sunbeam wraps around my heart,
As I slide down verbal hills,
Savoring the laughter of life,
In windswept jests and thrills.

Fierce Ink

With a pen in hand, chaos reigns,
My words take flight like runaway trains.
They dance and twirl, defy all sense,
Every line's a wild recompense.

A cat in a hat leaps on the page,
While socks on a rooster ignite a rage.
Scribbles and giggles lead the way,
In this ink-filled circus, we'll laugh and play.

Unbound Expressions

A chicken draws pictures with its beak,
While a fish in a tux says, "Now that's unique!"
Each doodle wrestles, both clumsy and free,
In this zany realm of creativity.

A turtle in sneakers races a hare,
Who forgot he's got wings and is flying through air.
With colors and quirks, we spill and we splash,
Alive with the laughter, a shimmering clash.

Rhapsody of the Unrestrained

Giraffes in bowties doing the cha-cha,
While elephants twirl like they're in a gala.
Every squiggle sings a silly tune,
As rainbows take flight like a hot-air balloon.

Frogs croak sonnets while wearing a crown,
And the moon giggles, wearing a frown.
This rhapsody's wild—a kaleidoscope sight,
Where nonsense ignites pure delight!

Vagabond Verses

A suitcase travels with legs of its own,
Hitchhiking a ride on a whimsy-zoned throne.
With mismatched buttons and jumbled seam,
It tells of adventures in a daydream's gleam.

A wayward sock wanders off in the night,
Searching for mates with all of its might.
In this world of oddballs, let laughter flow,
As vagabond verses steal the show.

Untrodden Paths of Poetry

In a field where ducks can dance,
The rhymes take a silly stance.
With wobble in each clumsy step,
They laugh, they quack, no need for prep.

A cat in boots, a hat too wide,
Sings ballads on a merry ride.
While juggling fish and zany frogs,
They cheer and chant through misty bogs.

The ink spills out in funny shapes,
As poets dream of paper capes.
With every word a bouncing kite,
They soar through clouds and laugh with light.

So take a stroll on paths untried,
Where giggles dwell, and puns abide.
In every line, a joke to share,
In this wild world, beyond compare.

Harmonious Havoc

A chicken plays the tambourine,
While goats compose a bluesy scene.
The cows join in with splendid moos,
Creating chaos, rhythm, and hues.

Jazz cats twirl in moonlit streets,
With silly hats and dancing feet.
They steal the show with feline grace,
Painting smiles on every face.

In a whirl of mismatched socks,
The rabbits crew, they twist like clocks.
With every hop and pounce they make,
Harmonies and giggles shake.

So clap your hands and stomp your feet,
Create a rhythm, feel the heat.
In this delightful, wild parade,
Join the chaos; don't be afraid!

Verses that Defy

A pickle waltzes on a plate,
Defying norms, it laughs at fate.
With every twirl, its brine does splash,
While dancing bread sings with a crash.

Old socks debate in silly tones,
Discussing cheese instead of bones.
They argue loud, they laugh and jest,
In this grand debate, who's the best?

With wild words that flip and flop,
The phrases spin, they twirl and hop.
Each stanza breaks the silly mold,
As laughter spills like tales retold.

From nonsense springs the fun we crave,
In verses dancing, mischief's wave.
So join the ride, let chaos reign,
In playful lines, we'll entertain!

Rhymes of the Restless

A rubber chicken walks at night,
With dreams of comedy in sight.
It tells of tales, both weird and wild,
As giggles echo, free and styled.

With roller skates on ketchup cans,
They dodge the pies and leap like fans.
Jumping jellies, in silly glee,
Bring laughter forth, oh can't you see?

A fish in glasses starts to sing,
Of octopus and other things.
With every note, the room ignites,
Filling hearts with sheer delights.

So here's to times of joyful quests,
Where laughter blooms and spirit rests.
In rhymes that bounce and never cease,
We find our joy, our happy peace.

Uncharted Stanzas

In a world of spoken rhymes,
Cat danced with squirrels and dimes.
Said, 'Let's write on clouds today,'
While the sun just laughed away.

Penguins wore hats, so grand,
As they waddled on the sand.
Chickens tried to fly, you see,
Clucking tunes of jubilee.

Lyrics of the Free Spirits

A goat sang high atop a hill,
Chased by chickens, what a thrill!
The cows joined in with moos and claps,
Making music with their naps.

The frogs croaked out a funny tune,
Dancing round a silver spoon.
While rabbits twirled with glee and might,
Underneath the starry night.

Echoes from the Wilderness

The owls hooted jokes at dawn,
While the deer dressed up in fawn.
Squirrels debated who was best,
In a mini tree-top fest.

Raccoons stole the spotlight bright,
Underneath the pale moonlight.
Their band played tunes from moonlit garbage,
A sound that brought no one a marriage!

Rhapsody of the Unfettered

A parrot squawked a silly play,
As the hippos joined in the fray.
Laughing hard in muddy pools,
Making fun of swimming fools.

The party raged in the trees,
Bouncing with the wild breeze.
Laughter echoed, sweet and light,
In that crazy, funny night.

Silenced Songs of the Bold

In the garden of jesters, they sing,
With rubber chickens and a rubber ring.
Their laughter echoes off the wall,
While the goldfish watches, standing tall.

In the circus of life, they dance and prance,
With silly faces, and a wobbly stance.
A tightrope of puns in the midday sun,
They juggle their jokes, oh what fun!

Yet, under the surface, a melody swells,
A forgotten tune amid prankster yells.
Silly hats concealing the brave inside,
With every giggle, they take in stride.

So let the songbirds join the spree,
In this land of laughter, wild and free.
For what's a bold heart without a tune?
Just a platypus in a bright balloon.

Raw Emotions in Ink

On a page where giggles meet the blot,
A quirky tale is what we've got.
With ink that drips in the wackiest way,
It dances like pasta, come what may!

The quills are shivering with delight,
As doodles take flight on a moonlit night.
Each scribble's a wriggle, a chuckle in lines,
A sonnet of shenanigans, laughter shines.

With a splash of confetti and a dash of cheer,
These raw emotions float, never a fear.
So spill your thoughts on the canvas wide,
Let chaos be your joyful guide.

Unruly hearts in a scribbled mess,
Find beauty in madness, who could guess?
As laughter tumbles from heart to pen,
Create a ruckus, then ruckus again.

Stirrings of the Unchained

In a world where socks never match,
The dreams are wild, a kooky catch.
With feathers and sparkles in every thought,
The stories unfold that life forgot.

Bouncing off walls like a rubber ball,
With giggles that echo and never fall.
Each mishap a dance, each stumble a feat,
Life's a hoot when you're light on your feet.

Chasing the moon with a sandwich in hand,
They skip through the pathways of the toppled sand.
For every zany thought that finds its way,
A laugh is a treasure that brightens the day.

So step out boldly, let the oddball reign,
In the gallery of quirks, it's never plain.
For in every chuckle, wild hearts remain,
Dancing on clouds, uncaged from the chain.

Lyrical Mavericks

They ride the rhythm of a bumpy beat,
With mismatched shoes and a heart full of heat.
Nonsense spills from their dreaming head,
As they paint the town with colors unheard.

Each verse a twirl, a wink, a grin,
With sassy remarks that make heads spin.
In the land of folly, they take their stand,
With pie in the face, it's all been planned.

So grab your hat, let the mayhem start,
These lyrical mavericks steal the heart.
Through laughter and chaos, their stories grow,
With humor and whimsy, they steal the show.

For in every chuckle, there lies a spark,
That brightens the shadows and chases the dark.
So join the parade, let your spirit soar,
With mavericks of laughter, who could ask for more?

Echoing Dreams of the Wild

In the jungle, cats do tango,
While the monkeys juggle mango.
Lions roar, their manes a mess,
Who knew wild could be such a guess?

Parrots squawk in socks and ties,
Kangaroos hop with alibis.
A zebra slips on sunflower seeds,
Life's a circus, amidst the weeds.

Baboons dance with wiggly glee,
A sloth joining in for a cup of tea.
The spider spins, wearing a hat,
Spinning webs with a silly chat.

Beneath the moon, the coyotes prance,
Chasing dreams in a silly dance.
The wild's a stage, where chaos reigns,
Laughter echoes in the hills and plains.

Unleashed Rhythms

Bouncing bears with disco flair,
Raccoons dancing without a care.
The owls throw confetti from high,
While squirrels attempt to learn to fly.

Frogs are croaking, keeping beat,
Pigs in tutus tap their feet.
Giraffes join in with a tall old tune,
While hippos groove 'neath the bright full moon.

Pandas munching bamboo with style,
Trying to dance, they slip for a mile.
The rhythm is wild, the beats so loud,
Making each animal feel quite proud.

Under the stars, the creatures sway,
In their own funny, silly way.
The jungle's alive with laughter, oh dear!
Where wild things dance and no one interferes!

Untamed Echoes

Echoes of laughter from trees up high,
Where squirrels hold a stand-up sky.
Rabbits joke in their own hare-raising way,
While turtles slow dance in the sunny ballet.

Chirping crickets form a band,
With grasshoppers lending a helping hand.
A wise old owl hoots a comic yawn,
As the sun sets on the outrageous dawn.

Foxes tell tales of mischief caged,
As the old badger feels quite enraged.
Raccoons share snacks with feigned dismay,
Turning nighttime into a wild buffet.

The shadows grow longer, fun's on the rise,
With gleeful whispers and goofy sighs.
Nature's a comedy, full of jest,
With echoes of laughter, we're truly blessed.

Verses from the Unconventional

In a world where penguins can twirl,
And beavers can give fashion a whirl.
Llamas recite with a flair for the odd,
While crocodiles nod in a wacky facade.

Otters crack jokes as they slide on land,
With turtles rolling out laughter, so grand.
A parrot reads poems of love gone awry,
While spotting a snail racing by on the fly.

Wombats break dance, giving a shout,
Bison join in, hip-hopping about.
The kangaroos bounce with a comical twist,
Life in the wild is a giggle-fest missed.

When night falls, and stars start to gleam,
Animals gather for their wildest dream.
In verses unconventional, they spin a delight,
Creating a world that's forever alight.

Chaotic Canvases

Splash of paint, a wild fling,
Colors dance, like birds on a string.
Brush strokes fly, the canvas yawns,
A masterpiece born from happy pawns.

Squirrels in berets, very chic,
Balance on ladders, oh so sleek.
A rabbit's hat, with feathers and flair,
Adds a twist, who put that there?

Kites in the sky, twirling by,
Chasing clouds, that sneaky pie.
Laughter paints each stroke we draw,
In this chaos, we find our law.

Every hue, a giggle in motion,
Creating art as wild as the ocean.
Forget the rules, let mayhem ring,
Join the fun, let the critics sting!

The Freedom Tapestry

Threads of laughter, weaving bright,
Hats on dogs, what a sight!
Twisted yarns of silly schemes,
Pillow fights and ice cream dreams.

Balloons fly high, tight with glee,
Dancers prance with cups of tea.
Lions wear ties, looking grand,
While hippos break dance on the sand.

Each knot a joke, each stitch a cheer,
Chaos embraced, there's nothing to fear.
Silly socks take center stage,
In this tapestry of fun, we engage.

The fabric laughs, as we all sway,
In this vibrant scene, we dance and play.
No dull moments in this craft,
Just silly giggles, our joy is daft!

Noisy Silences

In the quiet, a clatter grows,
A chicken tap dances on her toes.
Whispers loud, in hushed delight,
As mice hold a concert, oh what a sight!

Turtles strumming on guitar strings,
Serenading frogs with all the bling.
Crickets laugh, they steal the show,
In this quiet chaos, they steal the glow.

A lion snores, a thunderous song,
The silence bursts, it won't be long.
Socks in the dryer play hide and seek,
The noisy silence, it's truly unique.

Bubbles giggle, they float on air,
Every silence has a funny flair.
In the stillness, let laughter ring,
For within the hush, we all can sing!

The Pulse of the Wild

Beats of the jungle, rhythm and roar,
A parrot counts, 'One, two, and more!'
Tigers cha-cha, in vibrant bloom,
Dance to the frenzy, shake the room.

Bouncy kangaroos join in the fray,
Hip-hop moves, as they sway.
Monkeys juggling bananas galore,
Laughter echoes, we always want more.

In the wild pulse, giggles erupt,
Felines and canines blurring the cup.
Each heartbeat quickens, with joy anew,
In this free-spirited world, it's all askew.

So let's twirl and clap, dance 'til we drop,
In the wildest beat, we'll never stop.
As the forest sings, we'll join the fight,
For in madness, we find pure delight!

Rebellion in Every Line

A pencil rebel on the desk,
Scrawls a tale of thoughts grotesque.
It giggles loud at rules nearby,
And launches words to touch the sky.

Its ink spills stories, wild and free,
Like squirrels dancing on a tree.
With every stroke it breaks the mold,
A riot's heart in letters bold.

Censorship? It scoffs with glee,
A plot twist pulls the reader's knee.
It paints the world in shades of fun,
Turning blank pages into a run.

So grab your quill and join the feast,
Where laughter's reign shall never cease.
Let paragraphs of joy collide,
In written chaos, we take pride.

Tales from the Unfenced

A chicken dared to cross the road,
To find the world, a funny load.
It clucked of freedom, oh so bold,
While dodging cars—what a sight to behold!

Grasshoppers planned a wild parade,
With snacks of crumbs in the glade.
They jumped and danced, a hopping spree,
While ants just stared with envy, whee!

Squirrels played poker in the trees,
In windy gusts, they had great tease.
With nuts as chips, they rolled the dice,
And bluffed each other—it was quite nice!

The sun set low, the laughter soared,
As tales of mischief were adored.
In this unfenced world, so quaint,
Every creature dances—ain't that great?

Rogue Narratives

A cat wearing boots prowls around,
Wearing shades and looking profound.
It tells tall tales of kitty crime,
While swiping treats, oh what a mime!

A fish named Bob started to sing,
About the life beneath the spring.
With gills aflutter, he made a splash,
As bubbles rose in a bubbly clash.

A raccoon thief with a top hat,
He steals leftovers—just imagine that!
With sticky paws and a cheeky grin,
He winks at you, as he slips in.

These rogue tales keep our hearts alive,
In hilarious antics, we shall thrive.
So join the fun, don't be shy,
For every story lifts us high!

Call of the Untamed

A dog in a tutu prances with flair,
Chasing its tail as if it's not there.
With every spin, it woofs a tune,
Barking to the beat under the moon.

A goat on a skateboard zooms by fast,
Defying gravity, it's quite the blast.
It jumps and flips, the crowd's in awe,
While munching grass with deviant paw.

A parrot tells jokes, oh what a bird,
With punchlines sharper than any word.
It squawks of pirates in a comical jest,
Leaving its pals in laughter, impressed.

In this wild realm of joy and cheer,
Every creature lends an ear.
So heed the call of laughter's game,
And find your wild in poetry's name.

Songs of the Restless Soul

There's a squirrel on my roof, he sings all day,
Chasing down the birds, in a frantic ballet.
With a nut in his paws, it's quite the charade,
He thinks he's a star in the world's grand parade.

My coffee is dancing, it jumps from my cup,
While I dream of donuts that never give up.
The toaster is laughing, it burns every slice,
But every morning madness feels oh so nice.

In the Shadow of Freedom

The cat in the window is plotting a coup,
She stares at the garden like it's her debut.
With a flick of her tail, she claims all she sees,
While the goldfish just bubbles, feeling quite a tease.

A dog in a sweater, who's fancy and proud,
Struts past the pigeons, they gather in crowd.
He thinks he's a lion, majestic and bold,
In the realm of the asphalt, a sight to behold.

Unfettered Dreams

In my dreams, I can fly, but I trip on the ground,
Flapping my arms like a goofball unbound.
Bananas are taxis, they drive me around,
Through forests of candy, where laughter is found.

A fridge full of pickles sings songs to my brain,
While socks on the floor are plotting my fame.
They tell me I'm special, in a wobbly way,
But I'm still just a clown in this circus today.

Ballad of the Wildflower

A wildflower giggles, sprouting in cracks,
Sticking her tongue out at the passing tax.
With petals of purple and green sparkling bright,
She dances with bees, in the warm morning light.

She told me her secret of chasing the sun,
That life's just a party, and we're all invited for fun.
With the wind as her partner, she twirls with delight,
In a world full of chaos, she shines ever bright.

Words without Borders

Words travel fast, like a cheeky fox,
They hop over fences, and tickle your socks.
With puns that dance, and metaphors that prance,
They sneak through the cracks, with a mischievous glance.

A joke in the air, with laughter as fuel,
They shimmy and shake, breaking all the rules.
Spinning tall tales with a wink and a grin,
Each line is a passport, let the fun begin!

In rhymes that jive, and rhythms that swing,
Words become gems, oh, the joy they bring!
With giggles and chuckles, they tickle the mind,
In this wild word party, see what you find!

So gather your thoughts, let your tongue be free,
In this land of chatter, come laugh with me!
For every line penned is a ticket to cheer,
In the world of words, there's nothing to fear!

Ferocious Expressions

With a roar of laughter, they leap from the page,
Expressions that frolic, like a wild rampage.
A smile like a lion, fierce but so bright,
In the jungle of phrases, they take flight!

Each pun is a growl, each giggle a chase,
In the wild of the verses, there's no saving face.
With a wink of the eye and a playful shove,
These ferocious words fit like a glove.

Chasing the rhymes like a playful pup,
In this playful safari, who's ready to sup?
Gobbling each line with a joyous delight,
They pounce on your heart, oh what a sight!

With a twist and a turn, they dart through the air,
A family of words that are beyond compare.
So join in the fun, don't be left behind,
In this ferocious laughter, true joy we'll find!

Fugitive Footprints in Verse

Footprints of humor dance in the sand,
Leading to laughter, just grab my hand.
Their paths are a puzzle, a riddle untold,
With giggles a-whisper, they're daring and bold.

Like runaway socks, they vanish from view,
But follow the giggles, they'll lead back to you!
In the verse where they scamper, so free and alive,
Those sneaky word trails make joy thrive!

They skip through the grass, avoiding the rain,
In a merry parade, they cast off the mundane.
With every dash taken, a story unfolds,
In the chase of the laughter, the heart never folds.

So track those wild words, let them guide you right,
In this playful sprint, everything feels light.
For in every lost footprint, there's wisdom to claim,
In the laughter we share, love is the game!

Boundless Boundaries

Boundaries dissolve like ice in the sun,
In the realm of the quirky, where all's just for fun.
With a wink and a nudge, we tiptoe the line,
In this world of their making, our laughter will shine.

With doodles and giggles, they dance on the edge,
Pushing the limits, they won't budge or hedge.
In a whirlwind of whimsy, they break every chain,
Creating a circus in this funny game.

In haikus that wiggle and verses that gleam,
Each boundary they shatter fuels another dream.
With a hop and a skip, on the edge of absurd,
They turn life to poetry, with just a few words.

So join in this revelry, let your cares take flight,
In this land without borders, the future is bright.
For the laughter we gather knows no force to contain,
In this dance of the verses, we lose and we gain!

Cascading Verses

In the jungle gym of rhymes,
Laughter swings on monkey climbs.
Words bounce like rubber balls,
In a world where humor calls.

Slapstick jokes on dancing bears,
Cheetahs laugh while flipping chairs.
Puns erupt from slothful trees,
Tickling trunks with such great ease.

Tigers tell tales in jest,
While parrots squawk, they do their best.
Spinning yarns that twist and twirl,
In this merry, wild swirl.

So join the party, don't be shy,
In this verse, we all can fly.
With laughter loud and spirits free,
Let's cascade with glee—just you and me.

Harmony Amidst the Wild

In the choir of the crazed,
Every song a laugh is raised.
Meerkats strike a pose and sing,
Humming tunes like they're the king.

Baboons with hats, they hold a show,
Juggling fruit while stealing the show.
Rhythm shakes the rhythm of trees,
As nature giggles with the breeze.

A zebra dances, spunky and spry,
With polka dots that catch the eye.
Harmony found in wild delight,
With silly antics shining bright.

Together we're a singing pack,
Joking loudly, there's no lack.
In this wild, joyous embrace,
Funny tunes fill every space.

Declarations of the Ferocious

Roars of laughter fill the night,
A ferocious sight, oh what a fright!
Lions strut in silly shoes,
With trumpets blaring, they can't lose.

Crocodiles don't hide their grins,
As they boast of all their wins.
"Fear us not, we're oh so cute,"
They prance around in a funny suit.

Wolves make pacts on what's a joke,
Over fire, they puff and smoke.
"Let's howl at the moon, it's super near,"
With each chuckle, they bring good cheer.

Declarations of the wild and free,
Come join this raucous jubilee.
In this feral, funny dance,
All of nature takes a chance!

Wordplay in the Wilderness

In the heart of a bustling grove,
Puns and jokes begin to rove.
A squirrel shouts, "I'm nuts for you!"
While birds hum tunes, a froggy hue.

Grizzly bears wear glasses so fine,
Declaring, "It's time for a vine!"
Jumping from tree to laughing tree,
In this wild wordplay jubilee.

Elephants in colorful ties,
Cracking jokes beneath the skies.
"Don't be gray, join in the fun!"
Chirps and chortles weigh a ton.

Wordplay dances in every glance,
A comical juggle, an urgent prance.
In the wilderness, we all unite,
For a laugh as bright as the starlit night.

Poetry without a Leash

The poems run wild, like a dog at the park,
Chasing squirrels with glee, leaving laughter in the dark.
They trip on their words, fall flat on their face,
But bounce back with a grin, ready to race.

Rhymes jump and jive, like a cat on a spree,
Hitchhiking on rhythm, sipping tea by the sea.
They dance with delight, twirling on a whim,
Making fun of themselves, with joy in every limb.

Metaphors leap like frogs in a pond,
Croaking their tales, of a world so abscond.
They waddle and wobble, then hop without care,
Creating a ruckus, a lyrical fair.

These verses run rampant, no leash to restrain,
Like kids on a sugar rush, bursting with sprain.
Their energy spreads, like glitter in the air,
Making poetry a playground, if you dare.

Spirited Soliloquies

Words frolic and play, like kids in a field,
Chasing their shadows, in laughter they yield.
Witty remarks fly, like kites in the sky,
As verses are tangled, oh my, oh my!

With a wink and a nudge, the lines tumble down,
Wobbling like dancers, wearing a crown.
The meter gets dizzy, but who even cares?
In this circus of stanzas, there's joy everywhere.

Puns prance like deer, through the forest so bright,
Each one a mischief, a humorous sight.
On pages they giggle, in margins they roll,
Spirited whispers, that tickle the soul.

In this lively display, let laughter be heard,
As spirits collide with each jolly word.
The verses will sing, with a heart full of cheer,
Spirited soliloquies, crystal clear.

In the Heart of the Untamed

In jungles of phrases, the wild things run free,
Chasing all logic, in a raucous decree.
They swing from the branches, with metaphors tight,
In the heart of the wild, they frolic all night.

Syllables roar, like a lion with flair,
In this crazy safari, there's no need for a chair.
They pounce on their rhymes, with a playful demand,
In the heart of the wild, poems are unplanned.

With chuckles and snorts, the verses all play,
Like squirrels with acorns, they frolic away.
Witty and wild, they create quite a show,
In the heart of the wild, let the laughter flow.

Riding the rhythm, they gallop and glide,
With giggles and gales, there's nowhere to hide.
These lines run amok, in a forest of glee,
In the heart of the wild, come and dance with me!

Syllables of the Wild

Syllables prance like a puppy on grass,
Bounding and leaping, they never will pass.
With each little bark, they'll make you just smile,
Syllables frolic, with style and a guile.

Riding on rhythms like waves in the sea,
Each note is a giggle, each pause is a spree.
They bounce and they wiggle, like jelly on toast,
Syllables of the wild, we giggle the most!

Like kittens in boxes, they poke and they tease,
The verses get tangled, like shoestrings with ease.
They trip on the punchlines, they tumble and roll,
In syllables of the wild, they conquer the soul.

So come join the fun, let the laughter expand,
As we weave through this land, hand in hand.
These words take flight, like balloons in the sky,
In syllables of the wild, let our spirits fly!

Whirlwind of Verses

A squirrel wearing glasses, quite dapper indeed,
He reads poetry under the old oak tree.
Chasing his thoughts like a cat with a bead,
His laughter echoes, how silly and free!

With a hat made of feathers, he spins 'round and 'round,
Writing sonnets for flowers, quite fanciful fun.
The bees in a chorus, they buzz all around,
While he dances through rhymes like a jolly young son.

Roaming Imagination

A fish on a bicycle, what a curious sight,
Pedaling slowly through puddles of foam.
He hums to the stars, singing soft into night,
Dreaming of journeys far from his home.

A cat wearing boots, on a stroll with a mouse,
Together they search for the best bits of cheese.
They dance through the grass, yes, they're quite the pair,
Plotting great heists while they giggle with ease.

Unscripted Treasures

A crab in a tux, he's quite the charmer,
Inviting the beach to a grand little ball.
Shells glimmer and twinkle, it's no cause for drama,
Everyone's dancing, and having a thrall.

A duck that recites poems, such wisdom it shares,
While paddling gracefully, quacking with flair.
In this zany world, full of fanciful bears,
Even the shadows break out in a pair.

Nature's Untold Stories

A toad in a top hat, a gentleman bold,
Tells tales of the garden, both funny and bright.
With wit like a lightning bolt, sparkling and gold,
Each croak is a legend that lights up the night.

The flowers, they gossip, they wiggle with glee,
Sharing wild secrets that tickle the breeze.
And the sun, it chuckles, with rays full of spree,
In this whimsical land, even the air seems to tease.

Wild Whispers

In the jungle of socks, chaos reigns,
A lion's roar, but it's just my chains.
Monkeys swing with great finesse,
While I trip over my own mess.

Parrots squawk about my hair,
I thought I was cool till I became a bear.
Flip-flops flying all around,
I dance like I'm lost but still get crowned.

The winding paths of the living room,
Where vacuum monsters loom and zoom.
Chasing dust bunnies, I take my stance,
A grand ballet in my underpants.

With a grand finale of spaghetti night,
The sauce is flying! What a funny sight!
Feathers in my cap of wild delight,
Life's a circus, and I'm the spotlight!

Rhythm of the Defiant Heart

In the kitchen, the pots will clank,
I dance like a pirate, oh how I prank.
With forks for swords in a gallant fight,
A dinner showdown that feels just right.

The dog, my sidekick, joins the spree,
We waltz through chaos, just him and me.
The cat gives side-eye, utterly confused,
As we tango on counters, both bruised and amused.

A fridge full of treats, I take my pick,
Baking a cake, but it comes out sick.
Egg on my face, but still I cheer,
Life's a grand stage, and I'm the premiere!

With every stumble, I add a laugh,
Turning disaster to a joyful craft.
Heartbeats wild in a staccato spree,
Who knew chaos could set us free?

Echoes from the Unbridled Spirit

In a world of pillows, plush and bright,
I bounce like a floundering fish in flight.
Cushions stacked high, a tower of dreams,
I'm the king of my castle, or so it seems.

With giggles as fuel, my laughter's the song,
Bouncing off walls, where I feel I belong.
The wicked echo of a silly sound,
It keeps me dancing all around.

The fridge sings tunes of forgotten treats,
I dive for the cookies with acrobatic feats.
In a world of chaos, I carve my space,
Wearing sock puppets like a goofy embrace.

When my dreams take flight on a kite made of socks,
I laugh in the wind while the world's in a box.
With echoes of joy, my spirit runs free,
Life's a wild dance, just follow me!

Unchained Harmony

In a garden of weeds, I'm causing a ruckus,
Dancing barefoot, I look rather ridiculous.
With daisies in my hair and mud on my toes,
I sing to the beetles, striking a pose.

The chickens cross roads, what a peculiar sight,
They cluck and they strut, full of delight.
I join their parade, flapping with flair,
The world's our stage, no room for despair.

Kites fly high, dragging me along,
A tornado of laughter where I belong.
With every twirl that makes me dizzy,
I find my rhythm, life's getting busy.

In this symphony of glorious noise,
I'm a maestro of mayhem, empowered by joys.
So let the wild harmonies echo and sway,
In this unchained dance, let's seize the day!

Fierce Melodies in the Stillness

In the quiet, a rooster croons,
Hoping to catch all the cartoon tunes.
A dog dances, its tail swings wide,
While the cat just rolls, with aloof pride.

Squirrels debate, with acorns in tow,
Who's the wisest in the row?
The trees gossip, leaves in a spin,
As the sun chuckles, letting fun begin.

A frog jumps high, claiming the stage,
Wearing a crown, it's all the rage.
While crickets click a rhythm so loud,
Nature's delight, in dancing, they shroud.

Laughter escapes as bees buzz by,
Mocking the butterfly that's learning to fly.
A wild wind joins in, swirls laughter around,
In a concert of chaos, joy can be found.

The Dance of Unconquered Spirits

Beneath the stars, a raccoon prances,
Trying out all its wildest chances.
Fireflies twinkle with bright, cheeky flare,
While moonbeams laugh; it's a midnight affair.

Cats on fences, with a snarky sway,
Plotting their heists, come what may.
Sassy and bold, they leap and glide,
As shadows play on a magical ride.

Rabbits gather for a daring race,
Hurdling pots, they pick up pace.
The owl hoots in a fit of glee,
Watching the woodland, wild and free.

Every rustle, a giggle escapes,
In this loose world, nothing reshapes.
Sprightly and free, with a wink and twist,
Spirits dance wildly, none can resist.

Raw Cadence

A parrot squawks in quirky tune,
Mixing up words from morning to noon.
With every caw, it steals the show,
While the mice below steal crumbs for a growl.

Frogs in a chorus, off-beat and loud,
Croaking their way through a bumbling crowd.
Each splash is a giggle, a hop and a thrill,
They leap with fervor, no sign to be still.

Bouncing sprightly, a rabbit with flair,
Double-dutch flipping through the brisk air.
Its furry friends cheer, with little thumps,
As the chorus of chaos fills all the lumps.

Even the breeze can't handle the jest,
Tickling the leaves, it wants a rest.
In this raw rhythm, laughter prevails,
With nature's humor, the wildness sails.

Woven Threads of Rebellion

In the thicket, a story takes flight,
A hedgehog donned in a cape, what a sight!
Defending its turf with a poke and a wiggle,
While the badgers conspire with a raucous giggle.

Bumblebees buzzing, in choreographed strikes,
Dancing in circles, for daring delight.
Each flower a partner, sweet nectar's call,
In their buzzing rebellion, they conquer it all.

A mischievous fox leads a feathery chase,
With a gang of birds, it's a wild-foot race.
Through tangled paths, they dart and sway,
Crafting a ruckus, come what may.

Loud are the whispers of nature's decree,
In this threads' rebellion, all are free.
With laughter and jests, they break every mold,
Woven dreams dance, vibrant and bold.

The Call of the Untamed Night

In the moonlight, shadows dance,
Crickets chirp, and raccoons prance.
A daring cat on a fence takes flight,
Whispers of laughter fill the night.

Stars twinkle in mischievous glee,
While owls play cards with the bumblebee.
A squirrel spins tales, oh what a sight,
Boundless joy in the shadows of night.

Fireflies wink in dapper attire,
While frogs conduct a chorus of choir.
The breeze tosses giggles, wild and bright,
As friends of the night form a grand flight.

With every rustle and absurd sound,
The world turns flip-flops, loses ground.
In these antics, we find delight,
As laughter unfolds out of sheer fright.

Unruly Stanzas

These lines are ruling, no... wait, they're not,
A syllable slips and forgets its spot.
Words tumble out in a comical spree,
Like cats stealing fish, all wild and free.

Quirky rhythms skip and hop,
With frog-like choruses that just won't stop.
Nonsense marries a meter quite loose,
In the riot of words, we cut the noose.

Each letter's a jester, each line a clown,
Together they'd make quite the motley gown.
A pun here, a jest there, a rhyming delight,
In the chaos of stanzas, we take our flight.

And if one line stumbles or wobbles near,
We'll crown it the jester, let's make that clear!
For laughter is what fuels this mad spree,
In a world where norms can't maintain their decree.

Footprints on the Edge of Chaos

Tip-toe lightly on the chaotic brink,
Where giggles erupt faster than you think.
Each footprint a prank, a story untold,
In a landscape of mischief, daringly bold.

Bouncing off walls, like a rubbery ball,
With laughter that echoes, it answers the call.
Duck under the tables, swing from the trees,
In the mess of the moment, we do as we please.

Oh, the paths that we take are delightfully wild,
Like lost puppies foraging, unkempt and beguiled.
With laughter following, a jubilant chase,
We find joy in every chaotic place.

These footprints, they linger, tales of our fun,
The laughter, the shenanigans, never quite done.
In the chaos of life, we prance and we play,
With footprints that dance on the edge of the day.

Reverberations of the Unconventional

Sound the trumpet — a fish sings loud!
While squirrels compose in a quirky crowd.
Each note flips the world upside-down,
A symphony born from the circus town.

The cat plays the fiddle in a haphazard way,
While dogs jam along, needing to sway.
Their tails keep the beat, a clip-clop parade,
As laughter reverberates, chaos made.

An audience gathered of strange critters here,
With frogs in tuxedos sipping cold beer.
The scene? A circus of whimsical noise,
Where giggles and howls are the real joys.

So join the choir, the chorus of odd,
Where nothing is normal, and all's a facade.
In these echoes of laughter, we'll find our way,
In reverberations that brighten our day.

A Symphony of Rebels

They danced on rooftops, boots too tall,
With left feet fumbling, they'd trip and fall.
A kazoo band played, notes stuck in cheese,
Rebels intoning with giggles and wheezes.

Their hair sprouted grass, it rained lemonade,
While squirrels critiqued their wild charade.
With frying pan trumpets, they marched through the street,
Who knew that rebellion could be so sweet?

They formed a parade, all in mismatched socks,
Grit in their teeth, but laughter unlocks.
Sausage dogs dancing, the highlight of all,
Their symphony roared, a spontaneous brawl.

So raise up your glass, toast this foolish crew,
With giggles in hand, the mayhem is true.
A chorus of chaos, a riot of cheer,
In jumbled rebellion, let's raise a weird beer!

Words from the Wilderness

In forests where owls just can't keep the score,
They started a debate on who hoots more.
The raccoons were champions, they took the prize,
While squirrels took notes, with pierced little eyes.

An engine of banter, a stream of wild tales,
With dandelion ink and a chorus of whales.
They scribbled with branches, drew maps in the dirt,
And giggled as grasses played dress-up in skirts.

As night crept upon them, they lit up the moon,
With shadows and stories, they sang out of tune.
Voices like thunder, yet soft as a sigh,
Who knew the wilderness could make spirits fly?

So let's join their cabal, left foot in the air,
With hats made of leaves and a spark of a dare.
In the wildest of words, we find our bright road,
A merry discourse, where the laughter's bestowed.

Wild Reflections

In puddles we peek at our wild, twisted hair,
A mirror of mischief, a splash of despair.
We chase after giggles, as if they could run,
With apples on our heads, we play just for fun.

Our shadows play pranks, they leap and they dance,
Waltzing through puddles, they spin in a trance.
An echo of chaos in every hue,
Reflections of us, the goofy and true.

With leaves as our confetti and dirt as our gold,
Our wild little hearts could never be sold.
We scribble our stories in sand next to streams,
Embracing our nonsense, our dreams within dreams.

So here's to the laughter that tickles our souls,
To chasing the shadows and losing all controls.
In wild, silly ventures let our spirits sway,
In mirrors of mischief, we always will play!

Whispered Anarchy

In the quiet of chaos, whispers abound,
A rogue band of jesters break free from their town.
With noodle-wrapped hats, they conspire and plot,
To take over lunches and snacks they forgot.

Their voices like popcorn, they pop and they crack,
In secret convos, they plan their great snack.
With AI as their captain, they code their escape,
A mission for cookies, they'll never reshape.

They tiptoe on sidewalks, their giggles like grass,
While pigeons roll eyes and peek through the glass.
With every small whisper, their power's unfurled,
Anarchy's tasty, in this hungry world!

So raise up a kettle, let laughter steam high,
In whispered anarchy, we reach for the sky.
With breadsticks for swords and dip in our plans,
We'll conquer the playground with marshmallow bands!

Unscripted Whispers

In the garden, a squirrel scolds,
Telling secrets with acorn holds.
A rogue duck quacks a gossip spree,
While dancing grasshoppers scoff with glee.

A rabbit hops by, wearing a hat,
Claiming it's simply a stylish spat.
The wind giggles, tugging at my ear,
Poking fun like a cheeky deer.

A snake tries to tie up a shoe,
But slips and lands in the morning dew.
The daisies laugh, they just won't stop,
At a frog's failed leap from a bubbling crop.

So here we sit, sharing this mirth,
Nature's laughter, a joyful birth.
With critters and blooms all in a row,
Comedians unplanned, putting on a show.

Nature's Rebellion in Verse

Bees in bow ties, buzzing with flair,
Plotting their heist on sweet summer air.
While the flowers, in bright disarray,
Form a conga line, come join the play!

The trees swing their branches to the beat,
While ants march in, all tiny and fleet.
They've allied with the snails, all taking a stand,
Who proves that slow can still be quite grand.

A rogue wind nudges the clouds with a grin,
Shuffling them like cards, where to begin?
A rain drop rolls down and slips in the fun,
Joining the laughter, oh what a run!

Nature's a jest, a whimsical feast,
In this oddly chaotic, comedic beast.
So let's raise a toast to the wild and free,
Where laughter and greenery dance merrily.

Vibrant Chaos of the Uncontained

A pinwheel spins, on a gentle breeze,
While squirrels are plotting a snack with ease.
The daisies debate on who wears the crown,
As the sun rolls up, in her golden gown.

Butterflies argue their colors of choice,
Each flutters and flaps, raising their voice.
The blue ones insist they are best in flight,
While the browns say, "No, we own the light!"

A porcupine cracks a joke about spikes,
As hedgehogs giggle, amused by the likes.
And in all the chaos, the grasshoppers cheer,
At nature's mad party, their homey frontier.

So dance to the tune of this glorious mess,
With weeds in your hair, just do your best.
In life's vibrant chaos, let humor abound,
For simple delight is where joy can be found.

Wildflowers in Prose

Wildflowers whisper, a giggling spree,
Each bud and stem sings frivolously.
A bumblebee strolls with a fanciful grin,
Snagging a sip from where chaos begins.

The daisies are plotting a silly charade,
While lilies join in, their serenade.
With jokes about petals and who has the best,
In a world that's alive, they pass the jest.

Thistles grump, feeling quite out of place,
But all grass is swaying, keeping the pace.
A curious bloom tips its head to the sky,
Wondering why dandelions just fly by!

Nature's a play, each flower its role,
In petals and stems, a vibrant stroll.
So come join the frolic where laughs never halt,
In this wild, flowery, hilarious vault.

www.ingramcontent.com/pod-product-compliance
Lightning Source LLC
Chambersburg PA
CBHW070749220426
43209CB00083B/220